Cockatoo Calling

Story by Rebecca Johnson   *Photos by Steve Parish*

The Sulphur-crested Cockatoo was very upset. Some men were talking about cutting down the dead trees in the middle of the paddock.

He told his friend what
he had heard.

4

"We must
do something,"
they agreed.
They decided
to call a meeting
of all the parrots.

The cockatoos flew to the top of a tree and screeched as loudly as they could.

"My goodness!" squawked the Eclectus Parrot when he heard. "I'll be there."

"We'll come too," cackled the mob of Major Mitchell Cockatoos.

"I'll tell my friends," squarked the Superb Parrot.

Soon all of the birds were gathered at the meeting.

The Sulphur-crested Cockatoo proudly displayed his crest and told the others of his plan.

They all thought it was
a wonderful idea and
bobbed up and down
excitedly.

"We must save those trees," they agreed. "We need their hollow branches to build our nests in. People keep cutting down dead trees for firewood."

That afternoon they worked as a team.
The Palm Cockatoos collected palm nuts.

The Sulphur-crested
Cockatoos collected fruit.

The Rainbow Lorikeets collected flowers.

When everybody had collected something they flew to the trees. Some hid in hollow branches.

It didn't take long for the men to arrive with their chain-saws.

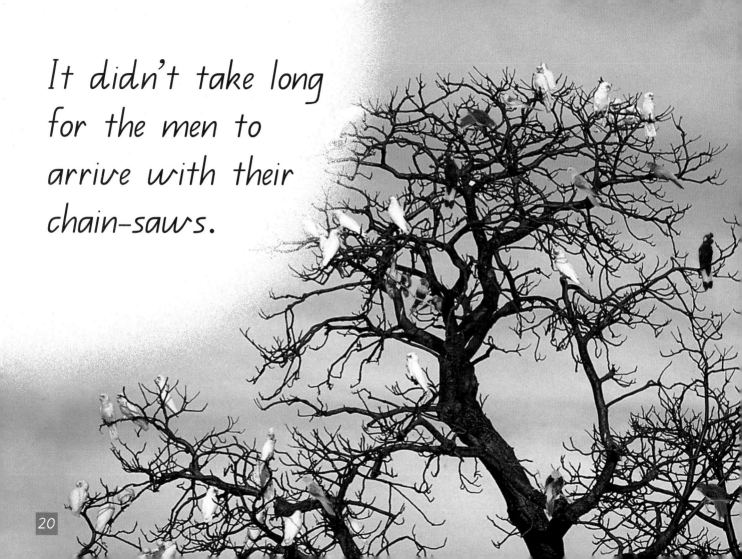

The birds waited until the men were right under the trees, then they screeched, "Get 'em!"

They dropped the fruit, flowers, nuts, seeds and twigs on the men, chasing them away and stopping them from cutting the trees down.

As the men turned to go, a cheeky Galah leapt into the air with excitement.

"And don't come back!" she shrieked.